The Body in Action

Eating

Claire Llewellyn

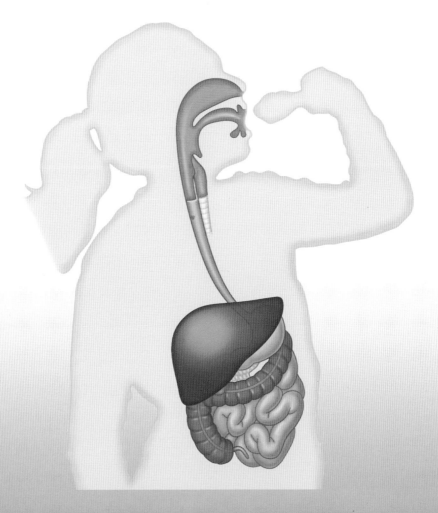

First published in 2004 by A & C Black Publishers Ltd.
37 Soho Square, London W1D 3QZ
This edition published under license from A & C Black Publishers. All rights reserved.

Produced for A & C Black by Bailey Publishing Associates Ltd.
11a Woodlands, Hove BN3 6TJ
Copyright © 2004 Bailey Publishing Associates

Editors: Alex Woolf and Jason Hook, Designer: Stonecastle Graphics, Artwork: Michael Courtney,
Picture research and commissioned photography: Ilumi Image Research, Consultant: Dr. Kate Barnes

Published in the United States by Smart Apple Media
1980 Lookout Drive, North Mankato, Minnesota 56003

U.S. publication copyright © 2005 Smart Apple Media
International copyright reserved in all countries. No part of this book may be reproduced in any
form without written permission from the publisher.
Printed in Hong Kong

Library of Congress Control Number: 2003063410

ISBN 1-58340-436-8

9 8 7 6 5 4 3 2 1

Picture Acknowledgements:
Corbis: 8; Nathan Benn: 15, 18; Mark E. Gibson: 28; Owen Franken: 22; **Getty Images:** Josef Peter
Frankhauser: 5t; Brian Hagiwara: 4; Philip Lee Harvey: 5b; Holly Harris: 29b; David Madison: 12;
Zul Mukhida: 24; **Science Photo Library:** 20; 29t; BSIP/Margiaux: 16; Martyn F. Chillmaid: 10;
Sheila Terry: 26.

Contents

Why you need to eat

YOU NEED to eat to stay alive. Food provides the energy you need each day to breathe, move, think, and stay warm. The food you eat contains **nutrients** that your body uses. Food helps you grow. It also helps keep every part of your body running smoothly.

Without plenty of food and water, your body does not work as well. Without any, it simply stops working.

This is a balanced meal. The fish provides proteins and fats, the potato provides carbohydrates, and the peas and carrots provide vitamins and minerals.

STAY HEALTHY
You should eat three balanced meals every day to keep your body stocked with enough food and water.

4

DID YOU KNOW?
Humans eat a great variety of foods. This is one reason why—unlike many animals—we are able to live all over the world, even in places that are very cold.

When you are very active, you need to eat plenty of food to keep you going.

People grow quickly in the first 20 years of life. Food provides the body with the nutrients it needs for this.

The food you eat contains different types of **nutrients**. There are foods for energy called **carbohydrates** and **fats**, and foods for growth called **proteins**. **Vitamins** and **minerals** keep everything working properly. To make sure that you get all of these nutrients, you need to eat many different kinds of food. This is called a balanced diet.

The digestive system

BEFORE FOOD can become useful to your body, it has to be broken into tiny pieces that are small enough to move through the body. In other words, your food has to be digested. The parts of the body that do this are known as the **digestive system**. This is a series of tubes and bags that mash up the food you have eaten and mix it with chemicals that help break the food down.

The useful parts of food, called nutrients, pass into your blood. Your blood then carries them around your body. Some food parts cannot be digested because they are too tough to break down. These leave your body when you go to the bathroom.

This apple is about to begin its journey through the body. The digestive system breaks the apple down into nutrients the body can use.

DID YOU KNOW?

Your digestive system turns all the food you eat into a soup-like mixture. Whatever you eat—hamburgers, strawberries, or chips— looks the same inside your stomach!

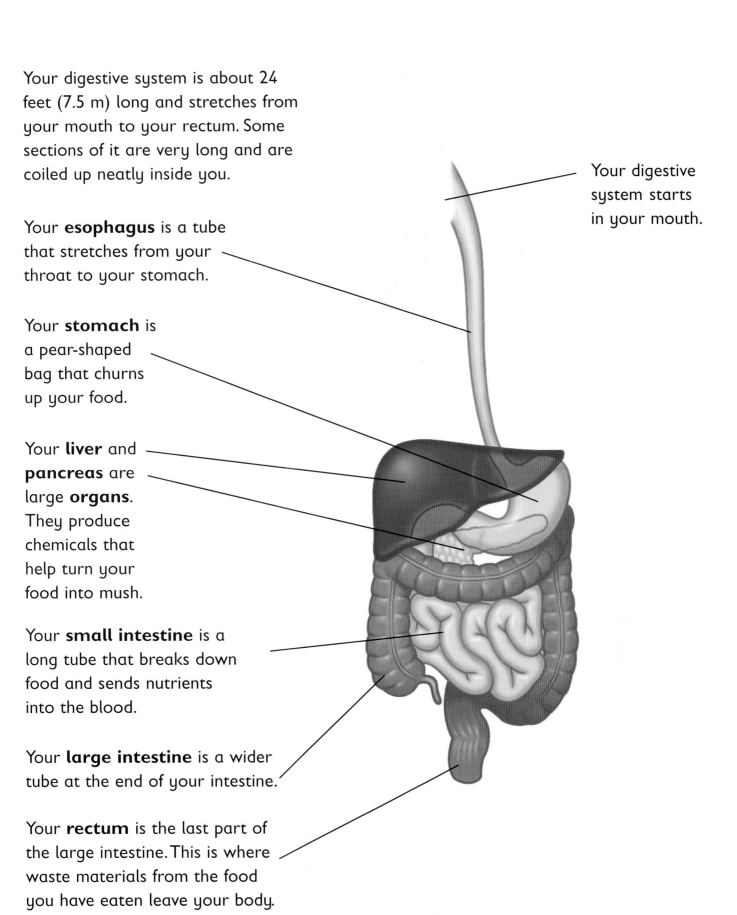

Your digestive system is about 24 feet (7.5 m) long and stretches from your mouth to your rectum. Some sections of it are very long and are coiled up neatly inside you.

Your **esophagus** is a tube that stretches from your throat to your stomach.

Your **stomach** is a pear-shaped bag that churns up your food.

Your **liver** and **pancreas** are large **organs**. They produce chemicals that help turn your food into mush.

Your **small intestine** is a long tube that breaks down food and sends nutrients into the blood.

Your **large intestine** is a wider tube at the end of your intestine.

Your **rectum** is the last part of the large intestine. This is where waste materials from the food you have eaten leave your body.

Your digestive system starts in your mouth.

Smelling and tasting

HAVE YOU ever eaten a rotten egg or moldy bread? Probably not. That is because your eyes and nose tell you that the food is bad. They do this to protect you from food that can make you sick.

When your stomach is empty, it shrinks and tightens. This creates a feeling we call hunger. It is like an alarm bell telling you to eat.

Your sight and smell also tell you when food is good to eat. Then your mouth starts to make a clear liquid called saliva to help make your food moist and easier to eat. But there is one last check your senses make before you swallow any food. **Taste buds** on your tongue check what the food in your mouth tastes like and warn you if it is bad. If you take a mouthful of sour milk, you still have time to spit it out.

DID YOU KNOW?
The senses of smell and taste are closely linked. When you have a cold, your sense of smell is so poor that you can hardly taste your food.

When your nose, eyes, and tongue have told you that food is good, saliva pours into your mouth and starts digestion.

There are thousands of taste buds on the surface of your tongue. Their job is to detect flavor. Different areas of the tongue detect different flavors.

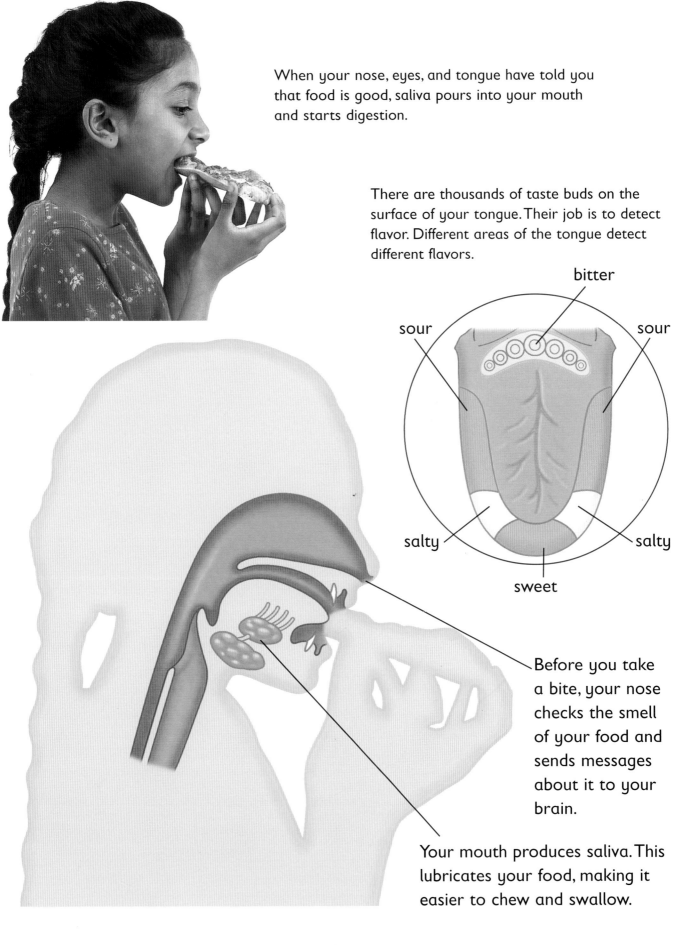

bitter

sour

sour

salty

salty

sweet

Before you take a bite, your nose checks the smell of your food and sends messages about it to your brain.

Your mouth produces saliva. This lubricates your food, making it easier to chew and swallow.

Chewing your food

WHEN YOU take a bite of food, your mouth breaks it down so you can swallow it. Hard, white teeth along your jaws cut, tear, and crush the food, mashing it to a pulp. Your tongue is a powerful muscle that rolls the food around your mouth and mixes it with saliva.

Your teeth, tongue, and saliva work closely together. In less than a minute, they have mashed that mouthful of food into a soft, slippery ball. Your tongue then pushes it toward the back of your mouth. There, the throat muscles squeeze it into the esophagus, and the food is swallowed.

STAY HEALTHY
Teeth are damaged by sugar. Protect them by brushing your teeth, visiting the dentist, and cutting down on sugary foods.

Sugary foods can damage your teeth and cause the formation of plaque. This is a film on teeth in which germs can live and spread.

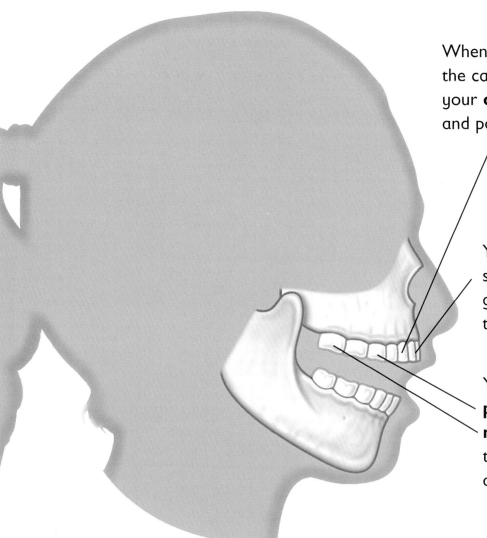

When you bite into a carrot, the carrot is gripped and torn by your **canines**, which are sharp and pointed.

Your **incisors** have sharp, straight edges. They are good for slicing and cutting the carrot.

You also have small **premolars** and larger **molars**. These broad, flat teeth are used for chewing and grinding.

You use different types of teeth to help break down food for swallowing. Each type has a different shape and a different use.

DID YOU KNOW?
A circle of muscle inside your lips helps to seal your mouth. This keeps water and half-chewed food from falling out of your mouth!

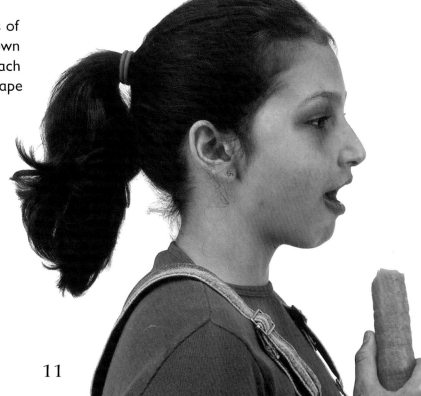

Digesting

OOD THAT has been swallowed soon travels to your stomach. This is a large, stretchy bag that works like a food mixer. It churns up the food with strong digestive juices. These help to break the food down into a thick, sticky "soup."

This soup is squirted, little by little, into the small intestine. Here, more juices from the liver and the pancreas continue to digest the food. Finally, after eight hours or more, the sloppy mix is broken down into tiny parts that your body can absorb.

DID YOU KNOW?

Your intestines squeeze food through the digestive system a bit like toothpaste being squeezed along a tube.

Your stomach needs time to digest a meal before you go for a swim.

STAY HEALTHY

Eating quickly makes your stomach produce a lot of digestive juices. This can give you a stomach ache. You can avoid this by eating slowly and chewing each mouthful well.

The first job of your digestive system is to break down food using strong digestive juices from several parts of your body.

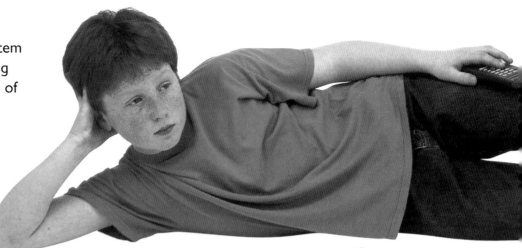

As you swallow, your esophagus squeezes food down to your stomach.

2-3 seconds

Your stomach is a bag with thick, muscular walls. It mashes up the food and mixes it with digestive juices. The time it takes depends on the type of food.

2-6 hours

Now the food is squirted into your small intestine. More digestive juices break down nutrients in the food until they are small enough to pass through its walls and into your bloodstream.

1-4 hours

Your liver produces a digestive juice that helps to break down fats.

Your pancreas produces a powerful digestive juice that flows into the small intestine. It contains chemicals that break down the nutrients in food.

The second job of your digestive system is to soak up water from the food and reject what is left.

The walls of your large intestine absorb water from the remains of your food so that what is left becomes more solid.

12-24 hours

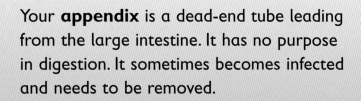

Your **appendix** is a dead-end tube leading from the large intestine. It has no purpose in digestion. It sometimes becomes infected and needs to be removed.

Your rectum stores the waste that is left over until you go to the bathroom.

2-5 hours

When all the nutrients have passed through the walls of your small intestine, a sloppy soup still remains. This is made up of the parts of the food that your body can't use. These now enter your large intestine.

The waste moves along very slowly. As the waste moves, the walls of the large intestine soak up its water. This leaves the waste drier and more solid. Finally, 18 to 36 hours after eating your meal, what's left of the food arrives in your rectum. It is stored here until you get rid of it by going to the bathroom.

STAY HEALTHY
If your large intestine becomes infected, you can get diarrhea. This makes you go to the bathroom a lot and makes your body's waste very watery. It is important to drink water to replace the liquid your body has lost.

Your digestive system works more smoothly if your food contains **fiber**. Fiber is found in fruit, vegetables, and wholewheat bread and cannot be digested. Its job is to add bulk to your food, helping it to move more easily.

A baked potato

POTATOES CONTAIN **carbohydrates**, which help to give you energy. However, carbohydrates need to be digested before they can enter the body. They have to be broken down into a simple form that your body can absorb.

There are two kinds of carbohydrates: sugary ones that are found in cakes and soft drinks, and starchy ones that are found in bread, pasta, and potatoes.

DID YOU KNOW?

Long-distance runners eat plenty of carbohydrates a few days before a race. The extra fuel keeps their muscles going longer and helps them run faster on race day.

STAY HEALTHY

Try to eat starchy rather than sugary carbohydrates. They give you energy for longer and do less harm to your teeth.

Pasta is a great source of starchy carbohydrates. After eating pasta, you won't feel hungry again for hours.

A baked potato contains starchy carbohydrates. These are quickly and easily digested to give you energy.

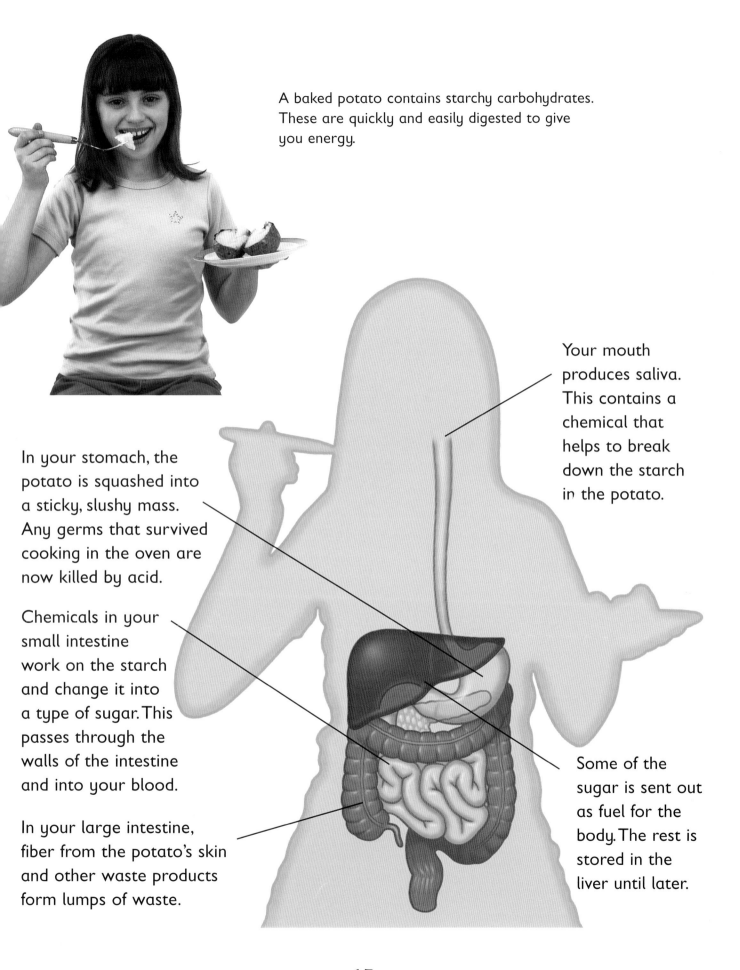

Your mouth produces saliva. This contains a chemical that helps to break down the starch in the potato.

In your stomach, the potato is squashed into a sticky, slushy mass. Any germs that survived cooking in the oven are now killed by acid.

Chemicals in your small intestine work on the starch and change it into a type of sugar. This passes through the walls of the intestine and into your blood.

In your large intestine, fiber from the potato's skin and other waste products form lumps of waste.

Some of the sugar is sent out as fuel for the body. The rest is stored in the liver until later.

A chicken drumstick

CHICKEN CONTAINS proteins and fats. The fats are found mainly in the skin, and the proteins in the meat. Proteins help the body to grow and repair damage. They also help to replace worn-out parts. Fats give you energy and help you to grow.

Proteins and fats are complex nutrients and are tricky to digest. Proteins are made up of smaller substances that need to be broken down before your body can use them. Proteins and fats are important nutrients, but you need to eat only a small amount of them to get the goodness they provide.

STAY HEALTHY
Try to eat two helpings of protein-rich food every day. Your body cannot store proteins, so you need a regular supply.

Proteins are found in both plant and animal products. Plants with a lot of protein include grains, beans, nuts, and seeds. Animal foods include meat, fish, eggs, cheese, and milk.

DID YOU KNOW?
Fats are found in animal foods such as meat, eggs, and milk. They are also in plants, but in plants they are called oils.

A chicken drumstick contains both proteins and fats. These nutrients take a long time to digest.

In your mouth, the chicken is chewed and mixed with saliva. It becomes soft, moist, and easy to swallow.

Your stomach grinds the chicken into mush. Chemicals break down the fats and proteins into separate, simpler parts.

Inside your small intestine, digestive juices change the fats into tiny droplets. The proteins are also broken down into smaller parts. The nutrients can now pass through your small intestine's walls and seep into your blood.

Water is absorbed from the waste that is left in your large intestine.

Blood containing the nutrients passes into your liver. Here the proteins are changed into new substances to help your body grow and repair itself. The fats are stored or sent out as fuel for your body.

Fruit and vegetables

RUIT AND vegetables contain lots of vitamins and minerals, which are very important for your body. Vitamins are chemicals that prevent disease and help the body work properly. Some vitamins are made by the body itself, but others come from your food.

Minerals, such as **calcium** and **iron**, are tiny substances taken up from the soil by plants. Whenever you eat plants (or animals that feed on them), you eat the minerals they contain. Like vitamins, minerals help your body work properly.

Vitamins and minerals are very important, but you need them only in tiny amounts. They do not need digesting and can pass straight into your blood.

STAY HEALTHY
Try to eat five helpings of fruit and vegetables every day. They can be fresh, canned, frozen, or in juice form.

Fresh fruit and vegetables are packed with vitamins and minerals. The sooner you eat them after they have been picked, the better they are for you.

DID YOU KNOW?
You can fit all the vitamins that you need each day on less than one-eighth of a teaspoon.

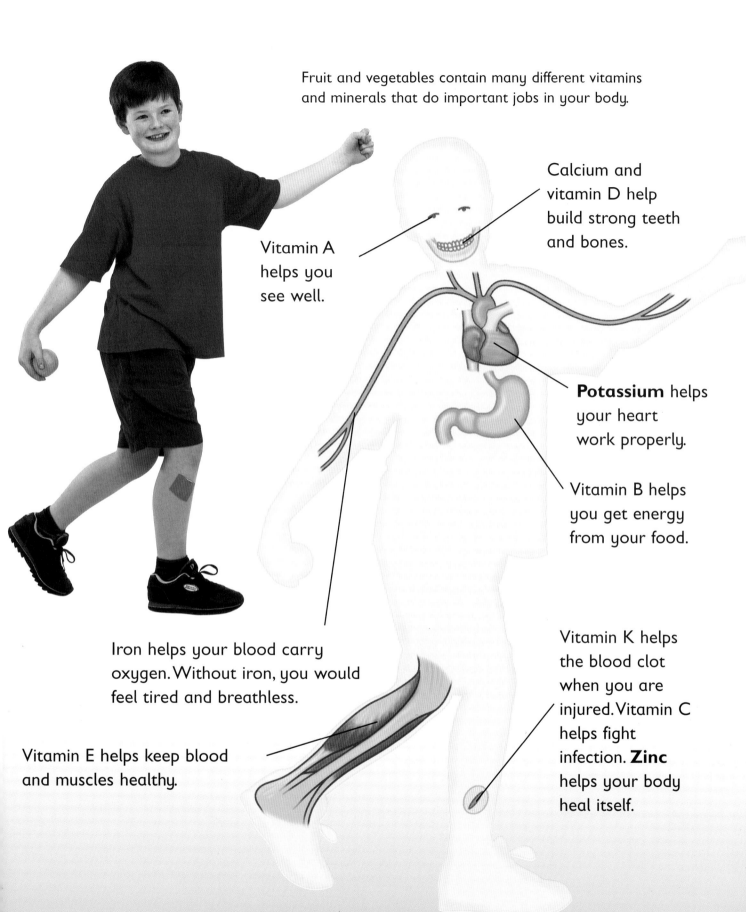

Fruit and vegetables contain many different vitamins and minerals that do important jobs in your body.

Calcium and vitamin D help build strong teeth and bones.

Vitamin A helps you see well.

Potassium helps your heart work properly.

Vitamin B helps you get energy from your food.

Iron helps your blood carry oxygen. Without iron, you would feel tired and breathless.

Vitamin K helps the blood clot when you are injured. Vitamin C helps fight infection. **Zinc** helps your body heal itself.

Vitamin E helps keep blood and muscles healthy.

A glass of water

WATER IS very important for your body. In fact, you cannot live without it. It makes up more than half your body weight and forms the liquids inside you, such as sweat and blood.

Water does not need to be broken down inside your body. When you take a gulp of water, it passes straight through your stomach and into your small intestine. When it reaches your large intestine, it passes into your blood.

Blood flows around your body all the time. Every few minutes it arrives at your **kidneys**. The job of your kidneys is to clean your blood by taking out the waste and excess water that your body does not need. This becomes a liquid called **urine**. Urine is stored in your **bladder** until you go to the bathroom.

People sweat a lot when they exercise. Sweat keeps the body cool and is 99 percent water.

STAY HEALTHY
You lose water when you breathe, sweat, and go to the bathroom. You have to replace it by drinking plenty of water—about eight glasses a day.

Water passes quickly through your digestive system and into your blood.

Water passes straight into your blood from the large intestine. This blood flows to your kidneys.

Your kidneys filter the blood. They take out waste products and any extra water. The liquid waste, called urine, now flows into your bladder.

Blood that has been cleaned of waste products leaves your kidneys and flows around your body.

Your bladder muscles relax when you go to the bathroom.

Your bladder gradually fills up with urine. It needs emptying three or four times a day. You do this when you go to the bathroom.

23

Being careful with food

FRESH FOODS such as meat, fish, and cheese are healthy and delicious. But they are easily spoiled by tiny creatures that live on them. These creatures are too small to see, but they are everywhere—on your hands, in the air, and on the things you touch. Some are kinds of **funguses** that make food moldy. Others are harmful bacteria or **germs** and can make you sick.

Germs spread quickly in places that are warm, damp, or dirty. They spread more slowly in the cold. That's why fresh foods should be kept in the refrigerator. Washing your hands and keeping the kitchen clean are other ways to stop germs from spreading.

DID YOU KNOW?
Bacteria are not always harmful. Certain good bacteria are added to milk to turn it into yogurt. These bacteria help us to digest our food better.

Fungus on this fruit is making it moldy. Food like this is bad to eat and should be thrown away.

Dirty cutting boards, work surfaces, and kitchen utensils can spread germs to food. Make sure they are clean before you use them.

Germs spread quickly on damp, dirty dish towels. Only use a dish towel if it is clean and dry.

Mold is a fungus that spreads through the air and feeds on your food. Eating it can make you sick, so throw moldy food away.

Washing your hands is important. It stops germs from spreading and prevents the illnesses they cause.

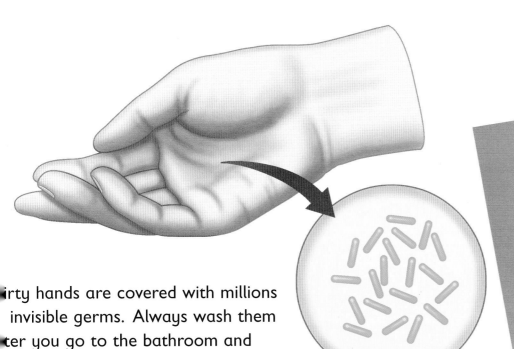

irty hands are covered with millions invisible germs. Always wash them ter you go to the bathroom and fore you touch any food.

STAY HEALTHY
Always keep food covered. This keeps flies from landing on it. Flies feed on dog droppings and dead animals and carry lots of germs.

Food allergies

SOMETIMES YOUR body reacts badly to certain foods. This is called a food **allergy**. The body mistakes the food for a harmful substance and reacts to fight it. This can cause skin rashes, sickness, or diarrhea. At its worst, the reaction can be life-threatening.

People do not always know which food is causing the reaction. Doctors find out by doing skin tests. They make a row of tiny pinpricks on your body and inject small amounts of suspect foods. If you are allergic to one of the foods, the pinprick will swell and turn red. This means you must not eat that food again. It can be hard in the case of milk, eggs, wheat, or nuts, because they are used in many foods. Children may not be able to eat food at parties because it might make them sick.

STAY HEALTHY

If you have a bad allergic reaction to a food, you may need medicine or an injection from a doctor. Some people carry their own injection kits to use in an emergency. If anyone you know has a bad reaction to food, dial 911 and ask for an ambulance.

Wheat, nuts, milk, eggs, and seafood are some of the foods that can cause an allergic reaction.

DID YOU KNOW?

Nuts can cause powerful allergic reactions. That is why packages carry a warning label to tell you if the food inside may contain traces of nuts.

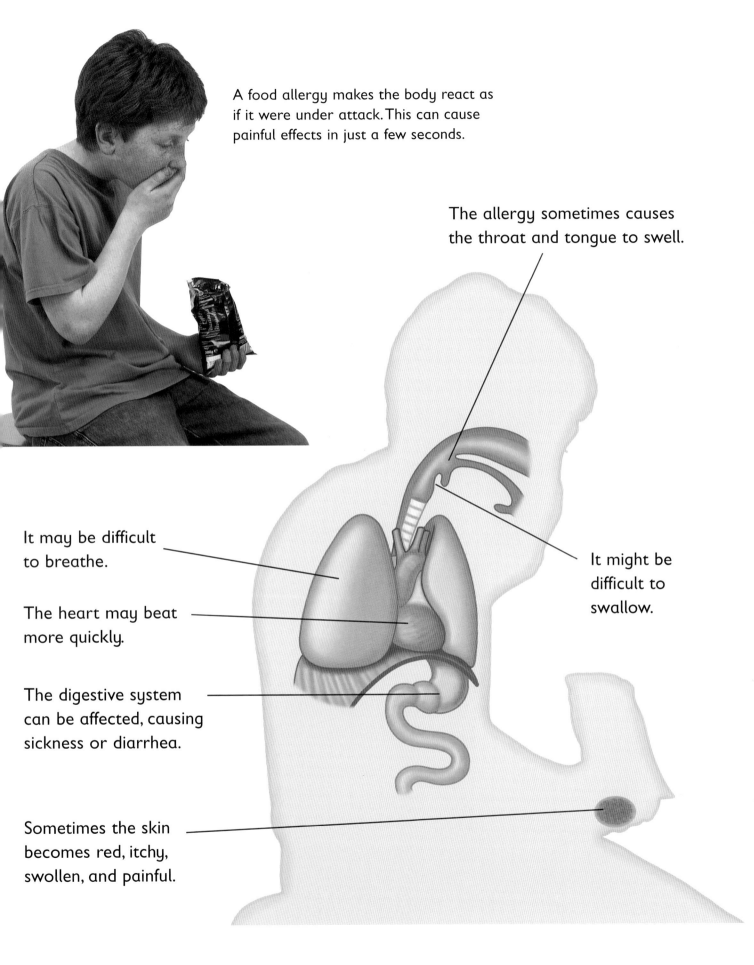

A food allergy makes the body react as if it were under attack. This can cause painful effects in just a few seconds.

The allergy sometimes causes the throat and tongue to swell.

It may be difficult to breathe.

The heart may beat more quickly.

The digestive system can be affected, causing sickness or diarrhea.

It might be difficult to swallow.

Sometimes the skin becomes red, itchy, swollen, and painful.

Healthy eating

Y OUR BODY needs many different nutrients. You can get them all only by eating a variety of foods as part of a balanced diet. It is best to avoid too many sugary foods, such as cookies and sweets, because they can rot your teeth. You should also avoid too many fatty foods, such as pizzas and chips. It won't hurt you to eat them now and then, but too many can make you fat.

Everyone needs to eat the right amount of food for their own body. Children need to eat more than older people. A big person usually needs to eat more than a small person. Eating too much can make you overweight. Eating too little will starve your body of the nutrients it needs.

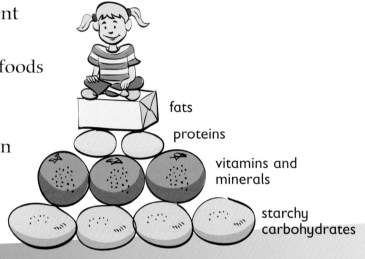

fats

proteins

vitamins and minerals

starchy carbohydrates

STAY HEALTHY

This food pyramid shows all the foods and nutrients your body needs. You should eat plenty of the foods at the bottom of the pyramid but only a little of the ones at the top.

It is easy to eat plenty of different foods on a picnic. Choose juicy strawberries and grapes as well as sandwiches and chips.

Fruit and vegetables provide you with vitamins, minerals, and fiber.

Milk supplies your bones and teeth with calcium.

Try to eat many different kinds of food. They are good for you in different ways.

Meat, fish, eggs, and nuts contain proteins.

Bread, cereals, pasta, and rice contain carbohydrates.

DID YOU KNOW?

You don't have to eat meat to get all the protein and iron you need. You can get protein from beans, chickpeas, lentils, milk, cheese, and eggs. Iron can be provided by spinach, broccoli, and other leafy greens, and by dried fruits.

A gooey cake makes a delicious treat. We all love foods like this now and then!

Glossary

allergy A reaction by your body to a particular food. It may cause sickness.

appendix A short, dead-end tube off your large intestine. It has no purpose in digestion.

bacteria Tiny living things that are too small to see. Some have useful roles in the body, but others can make you sick.

bladder A bag-like organ where urine is stored.

calcium A mineral in foods such as milk and cheese. It helps to build strong bones and teeth.

canine Any of the four sharp, pointed teeth near the front of your mouth.

carbohydrate A nutrient that gives your body energy. It is found in starchy or sugary foods such as bread, pasta, rice, and sweets.

digestive system A series of tubes and bags that break down the food you eat so that it can be used by your body.

esophagus The tube that joins your throat to your stomach.

fats Nutrients that give your body energy. They are found in foods that contain oil, butter, and margarine.

fiber The coarse, thread-like bits found in potato skins, carrots, and other foods.

funguses Tiny living things that make food moldy.

germs Harmful bacteria that can cause disease.

incisor Any of the four front teeth that have a straight cutting edge.

iron A mineral found in foods such as spinach and liver. Iron helps your blood carry oxygen.

kidneys Two organs that turn waste products from your blood into urine.

large intestine The final part of your digestive system, where waste products become more solid.

liver An organ that produces a digestive juice to help digestion but also takes in nutrients from foods and releases them to your body.

mineral A substance such as calcium and iron that is found in the soil and the foods we eat.

molar Any of the broad, flat teeth at the back of your mouth that crush and grind food.

nutrient Any part of a food that gives your body the energy or goodness it needs to grow.

organ Any part of your body that has a special job to do, such as your liver.

pancreas An organ near your stomach that produces juices that help digest your food.

potassium A mineral found in foods such as broccoli and spinach. It helps keep your heart and brain healthy.

premolar Any of the small, flat teeth behind your canines that help to crush and grind your food.

protein A nutrient that helps your body grow and repair itself.

rectum The part of your body where solid waste is stored before it leaves the body.

small intestine The longest part of your digestive system, where food is broken down into useful nutrients that are then absorbed by your body.

stomach The bag where the food you swallow is mashed up and mixed with digestive juices.

taste buds The parts of your tongue that detect flavor in food.

urine The yellow liquid waste that is produced by your body.

vitamin A special substance found in food that your body needs in tiny amounts to stay healthy. There are lots of different vitamins, such as vitamin A and vitamin C.

zinc A mineral that helps your body to heal.

Useful information

Books

Parker, Steve. *Look at Your Digestion.* London: Franklin Watts, 1996.

Royston, Angela. *Eating and Digestion.* Oxford: Heinemann Library, 1997.

Toriello, James. *The Stomach: Learning How We Digest.* New York: Rosen Publishing Group, 2002.

Web sites

www.brainpop.com/health/digestive/digestion Information, including a short film, on the digestive system.

www.schoolmenu.com A fun and informative site with games, facts, and puzzles.

www.kidshealth.org/kid/body/digest/ Information, including illustrations, on the digestive system.

Index